Americana Blvd.

Several of these poems were published in N'Motions in 1998, the literary magazine of Liberty University.
Many of the poems were also in the limited edition book 'Teardrop City and Others' published by the author in 1998.

This book contains a high percentage of new material.

Dedicated to Catharine and Brianna,
you are my hero's.

To the Genesians, for all of your
brotherhood.

❖   *Fame*

I dropped a pencil
in the spotlight
and became a star.

When I bent to pick it up,
I mooned the world.

Americana Blvd.

The collected poems of Jason H. Derr

Jason Derr

Writers Club Press

San Jose New York Lincoln Shanghai

Americana Blvd.
The collected poems of Jason H. Derr

Published by Writers Club Press
an imprint of iUniverse.com, Inc.

For information address:
iUniverse.com, Inc.
620 North 48th Street
Suite 201
Lincoln, NE 68504-3467
www.iuniverse.com

ISBN: 0-595-09713-8

Printed in the United States of America

Contents

❖ *Christmas Eve, 1999*

Children at three A.M.,
timid like frogs,
posing their lives like
delicate china cups,
talk in hushed tones
about pain.

Two cups of coffee
and I'm buzzed,
pen scratching on paper force's me
to reinvent myself again.

Conversations ebb and flow,
main points surfacing
through a haze of blue tobacco-drained
smoke.

Jeremy lays out his arguments,
hoping for some sort of honesty.

Bartering for a reaction from the
circus clown.

Carnival rides,
Face paint
paraded onto sawdust paneled
floors hacked up into
yellow and black.

The clown, red nosed and loud
juggles into a corner,
his face paint chipping,

He justifies

'I'm hurt,
I'm scared'

and through his paint
wipes at his blood.

❖ *Remembering Catherine*

Can we forgive so easily,
when what we love is destroyed.

The enemy of my heart sits quietly,
wetting the end of his cigarette,
as he snorts his way through
a salad.

Can I hate?
Should I hate him?
I know these things would come
so very easily if I beckoned them.

Is forgiveness,
that quite place,
so easily attained?

❖ *Grandmothers, in the last day's of 1999.*

Grandmothers,
picking lent from oversized sweaters,
and cupping hands-to-ear
(to radio the world in better)
know where the cracks are
in our old houses and complain
about the drafts.

❖ *The Ghost Town
is Haunted*

It was a night for dancing.
Or at the least, for walking slowly
and deliberately along crowded streets.

I remember the blond first—
her dress drifting like a summer,
she danced with the older gentlemen,
light and heavy, alternating between
grandfatherly types.

The breeze was like a blues rift dream.

She smiled

In the crowd,
he danced with her,
(his long time bride),
Ebony on Ebony,

swinging her into his embrace.

Tasting their lips on each other.

And the conga line,
a little girl leading,
finding beats that only
a 4 year old can.

The rest of us just walked around slowly
—deliberately.
Pacing our selves out,
wrapped in the June's fog
of introspection.

❖ *The City with the Street*

There was this one girl,
walking in front of me,
drunk and lazy,
who had the appearance of rain.

A drizzle,
long and thin,
a storm front on her head.

Her eyes 'lite' with a fatigue.
Or loneliness
Or lost-ness

Her companion,
standing to her right,
was lonely and round.

When she danced for him,
in the street with the Blues Band,
it was less an act of seduction

but more one of silliness

or post-modernism.

They were both drunk.
And lazy
And lonely

❖ *The Smoking Room*

I asked in open honesty for the game plan
and then asked for a light for my
old man pipe.
7 people in a room with a candle.

Our pipes ate into the air as our
council debated the ethics of midnight.

We passed our pipes and cigarillos
and cigarettes and sang songs
of praise.

And we sung 'American Pie'
I hope my daughters have this song.
I hope my sons can find it.

Or its brother or its cousin.

Everybody should smoke

too much on some remote
far off Friday and sing songs
with good friends.

Our children should be taught this;
innocent nights in our secular lives.

All praise to our lord Jesus Christ

❖ *A Short Time After Coffee*

2:00 am
Thursday
The Fog curls around the bridge
like a small kitten.

We walk along the side
whistling at the trains that
'Clack-click' bye,
below us.

We discuss the poetic aspects of film,
and philosophy.

Scott is scared of the light reflecting
off the water.
Tim and I talk to the moon's reflection.

The coffee is just kicking in.

❖ *Poem for Scott*

The young harvest moon is returning,
the old summer moon is dying
in a flower bed of dreams.

The wind catches a bite and greets
like a puppy at Six AM.

The mountain challenges you
Inward/Outward
The orange explosion threatening
to consume the mountain side.

The puddles at our feet vibrate
with anticipation.

❖ *Of coffee cups, friends and tantrums*

Last cups of coffee,
the poet goes into his angry spiel.
Silent paintings listen from lost
green painted walls.

He hurls forward, pitching into fever,
his nakedness dancing internally.
Defending the dreamer who hopes
reality is not the awakening.

❖ *Americana Blvd.*

I.

Americana Blvd.

Home of the brave and stupid.
Clapboard houses line streets
of oppsolent poverty.

A pink flamingo in every yard
and 2.4 children mentally scared.

American dreams bought cheap,
on street corners and in the
prostitutes crisp-sheet beds.

'Next Exit. Next Exit'

Take a right here to see
the American Dream.

We painted it yesterday
on the backs of immigrants
and slaves.

We bought it off the slave ships
and from the gardens of
Puritan Pilgrims.

From the trophy room of the native warrior.

We bought it and shinned it
and put it on display.

Look at us!
Four wheels spinning on
Americana Blvd.

II.

I drive here!
My college-wheels dancing on the
black top of a thousand political
dreams.

An hour behind is my small town.
An hour ahead is the big city.

And here;
here is where I am,
the noon sun casting a clock-like
shadow of my car.

Four duct-taped boxes contain
my every childhood memory.
(Now for sale on the internet)

III.

An immigrants ocean.
Teamed with people and capsized
with dreams too few and too scarce.

In the north the German-traditions still
holds.
In Miami we all speak with a
Hispanic voice.
In the south our words are drawn out
with a sudden drawl.

The Irish have Boston!
The Italians have New York City!

Somewhere a black-man sues the KKK
for discrimination.

Like Paul, we are all things to all people.

IV.

The Harbor saint,
a virgin always,
stares down the river,
lighting the way.

'Welcome, my children' she says

    'Were hungry'
    'Were tired'
       The river's passengers cry to her.

'I know, my friends—come in,
I am the patron saint of America.
From here its one exit to the blvd.'

'I have Chinese food and German food
and Italian food and Thai and Greek and
Mexican.
Take the exit, children, take the exit'

'No' says the dreamers' enemy
There is no work!
There is no room!

They sob at these lies!

V.

John Doe hitchhikes,
looking in trash cans
and in the dumpsters behind
our favorite restaurants.

John Doe walks the train tracks,
at night,
where the wind tosses by too quickly,
an invisible man on
an undetermined path.

John Doe fishes his dreams from
his pocket
and wipes his ass.

VI.

In my home I have
a book of my grandmothers
favorite Irish fairy tales.

From the 'Old Country'

VII.

Chinese fire drill
on a hidden factory.
100 migrant workers
loose their taxed pay check
and go back home

Off Miami a mother
Crucifies herself for
her son.

In New York City a young cab driver
sends money to his mother,
back home

Were all just making a down payment
on the American Dream.

❖ *The Passion of Ordinary Things.*

In hindsight;
I don't know much
about this millennium.

But, starting in the 1930's
my grandfather played jazz
and wrote songs with my
grandmother.
They played on cruise ships,
and orchestras,

they even had their own band,

The Jimmy Michelback Orchestra

He went on to own a furniture store
and adopt three children

One was my aunt, the other my uncle;
the third is my mother.

More recently my mother and I have waged
wars in our own souls against our
depression.

It is a struggle I will carry for life.

On a note:
I should mention my father.
Jerry, a quite man,
the son of a family scared
by the Great Depression
and World War II.

He has been designing the same
house for 30 years.

He will never build it, it will
live in his early morning dreams
and on paper for the rest of
his life.

In his heart he is a sales-man
and a country-boy.

My sister plays the flute and paints.

My mother, after years of trying,
finally gave up on the piano
and now teaches Learning Disabled Children.

In elementary school,
I hated those tests,
the ones that examined your
IQ and learning abilities.

'Your smart'
they say
'but you have a Learning Disability'

They never tell you if that's supposed
to be an indication of a handicap
or a challenge.

Eventually I decided it was a challenge.

I graduated High School a year early.

A brief list of my hobbies:

1)   Old Time Radio shows
2)   Reading
3)   Writing
4)   Haunting antique stores on weekends

5)   Theology
6)   Rainy Days
7)   Shadows
8)   & Sun Sets

As I write this my waiter
hums a few bars of a
popular Christmas Carol.

On Thursday, last week, I wrote 3 pages.
Friday I went for a walk and, with our dog.
a one year old German shepherd mix,
chased frogs.

That night I dreamt of this girl
that I knew in middle school.
I remember how, in my youth
I would go to her church and
pray:

'Jesus, if this girl fall's in love with me
I'll never ask for any thing else again,
ever'

This, of course, defeats the purpose of
a incarnate God who desires interaction
with his children.

I'm still friends with her
and she still teases me about how I used
to follow her around

On my birthday she said
'it's been a long strange
trip honey'
Two weeks ago I saw a rainbow

People laugh when I say I've
never been drunk or used
narcotics

I'm against anything that interferes
with mans nobility by slowing our
minds and bodies.

Quotes I like:
- 'Hollywood love ain't real love'
- 'Give God what is God's and Caesars
  what is Caesars'
- 'Inch by inch life is a cinch, yard by
  yard, life is hard'
- 'The ocean is epic and I was just sitting
  on the shore'

The last one is mine,
the one before is from a child's book

that I vaguely remember,
so be careful it's copyrighted.

Most people believe man
is inherently good.
I'm still unsure about that,
I can't explain human selfishness.

A girl in California tells me she loves me.
I'm not so sure about that;
I think she just likes the idea of me.

So do I.

Some questions i like to ask:
·   Do trees dream?
·   Do children understand their super pow-
      ers?
·   What if their were no celebrities, and
      only we could disappoint ourselves?
·   Where do cow's come from?
·   Can we have more clowns?
·   Is science fiction?

We refuse to define love,
but with an increasing divorce rate,
spouse and child abuse rate:
Can we afford not too?

My grandmother is a poet and songwriter.
I love the story about how she met Kennedy
and Einstein.

and of course the one about Glenn Miller.

My father wants to live in a cabin
in the mountains of North Carolina
cut off from the rest of the world.

Once, in Lynchburg Virginia
I learned that graveyards are meant
to be played in.
(it's the best way to celebrate the life
of dead poets)!

Things I don't understand:
- The lack of Orson Wells movies for
rent!
- Love
- Hate
- Why the sky is blue!
- The double standard of being 'open
minded'!

My mother used to cry when I did

I never really knew divorced people
or their children until college.

At 23 I'm still a virgin and proud of it

I think love should be Epic and Real

Some times I walk in on my parents
as they make out in the kitchen

I have a plank in my eye!

Josh wants to read this at my funeral
(If I die first)!

There is final, absolute truth!

Today's date is Dec 8, 1999

This is the last line in a poem about
the passion of ordinary things.

❖ *Neon City*

Cobblestone pathways,
spider-webs of confusion,
Criss-cross the city so bright,
dripping smog filled brightness
into pools of shadow dreams.

The secret pathways run up the alleyways
into the dark catacombs of shadows
and its kingdoms.

Running deeper from the safe paths,
into the shadows of Goblin King origin.
Half of me convinced that this
Is the short cut.

I stop as the scream pierces the night,
like an ice knife
thrust into the soul of man
and twisted slowly

There is silence.
Not a noise is spoken
heard not are the usual utterances
of drunk men planning their excuses.

Here the light never reaches
it cannot pierce the blackness
that hangs over our heads like a black tar,
absorbing all good that touches it.

The body (mutilated)
reminds us of the spider-web kingdom.

❖ *Teardrop City*

I was sitting alone in Teardrop City
sipping on a bottle of cold wind
on the corner of two streets
who's names have degenerated into
'That old place' and 'Near the old store'
warming a park bench
with my ass tattooed to the seat

Taking out my self-esteem
I shake it a little and watch
how it bubbles and fizzles.

With a rising red alarm
I notice that it is
quite empty, and decide to
go get a refill.

I walk a third and a ½ blocks
and notice the house of a girl I once knew.
Seeing her in the window, posing like an angle,

I take it out and toss it up to her.

She catches it in mid-flutter
and plays with it until it beats
like an African drum on parade.

She toys with it,
biting it slightly,
tickling and rubbing it.

Then she tears it to shreds and tosses the
remains down to me
letting the wind carry the pieces like fragments
of a broken dream.

Catching the fragments I put them back
together
with duct tape and stash them awkwardly
back in my chest,
were they ache with arthritis.

I moved along the yellow walkway
letting my steps tap out a rhythm.
Smiling ever so slightly to cover the pain
that shows through like a black mark
on my soul.

I met a man who shook his head

and talked of foolish wisdom,
and spoke in gray tones
on the dangers of angry people.

I gave him my heart and he quickly
dried it out and pumped it full
of hot air and angry lies and half-truths.
He took my heart and ran naked through the streets,
screaming of its perception and wisdom.

But anger and hot air become lead if hidden in a heart,
and it sank to the ground and snagged on a tree
and deflated.

I took my heart and held it in the sun and cooked it
at 1000°—but it did not work.

I again pieced my heart back together using gum and spit
and hoped it would not tumble apart.

I walked along Lazy River and met a group of girls and boys
who took their hearts and played volleyball

by suspending their hearts in the air and batting
them over the net,
they claimed to wear smiles but spoke with
storm clouds.

I joined their game, letting my heart be passed
from hand to hand.
Each member had an equal amount of destruc-
tive time with it.
After smashing three hearts on my own
and enjoying one group heart smashing,

I noticed that my own lay in a jig saw puzzle
on the sand.

I scooped the pieces into a bag
and put the bag in the crotch of my pants
and tried to fix my heart from their.

And again it was torn and scattered and lost
to the night howling sky.

Running through back alley cat paths,
jumping up and down on an old
garbage pail that contained little bags of my
rage

I remember pausing.

I saw a man standing among the trash who was
better than the trash.
Yet he picked the trash up and took its filth to
himself,

leaving them clean

I gasped in horror as he took out their hearts
-and tossed them into the alleys piles of rub-
bish
and then gasped louder as he gave them each
a new heart.

He came to me,
his hands and head
and back and side
were scarred, torn beaten and pierced.

Blood dripped onto me as I reached to take his
hand.

He sighed as my heart,
gray and decaying
fell into his hands.
He didn't laugh or complain.

But only looked it over

and I winced as he noticed
every imperfection and flaw
every crack,
every hidden secret.

I force words through my parched and cracked
lips
'I give it to you, can you fix it'.

He smiled and tossed my heart aside
and took a new one out from under his
robe.

I saw its wholesomeness, it's perfection.

'For me' I ask.
In an unspoken answer that is more than words
he placed it inside my tin-man chest.

I paused
trying out my new heart,
feeling the cleanness of each beat.

I felt how it responded
to emotions, and thoughts
and feelings and art
and poetry.

I could only say this:
'Surely you are the Son of God'

❖ *Road Trip: New Orleans, '00*

On the radio,
between repeated chorus's
of ill-timed love

we learn how to
spiritualize our
colon's.

❖ *In Exile*

I'm
looking back,
at our phone call's
and ill timed letters,

as an experiment in friendship

I'm looking back,
on the arguments I posed
and the mild ramblings
about our lives

and loves

L leaves in a hurry,
one day,
packing her dreams into
a canvas bag

Charlie,

(who broke L's heart twice before I ever did)
saw her before Paris,
Tim and Scott saw her
in Virginia Beach

I want to hire skywriters

❖ *Jan 7, 2000*

Monday night,
coffee cups filled endlessly
and the beach call's to us

A police car follows for
a few blocks;
but turns away uninterested

> By the ocean
> I dream of sailing

Today I want to climb trees

❖ *Festivals*

Remembering home,
& the thanksgiving
with the three of us

It was the last time
I ever saw L.
The first time she saw Charlie
in a long while.

> Eventually the two of you
> claimed it was love.

> Eventually you decided you
> were wrong.

About what I said;
I have no answer
for that.
But I would like to see you again.

For thanksgiving.

❖ *The Ripe*

Sometimes;
Home
a collection of parted dreams
and childhood photograph's

some old friends you grow beyond
some you don't
some grow beyond you

and some you just know for
reasons you can't yet decide on

Some;
and these are the pastor's kids,
become more like brothers

At
Home
we fake a multitude of conversations,

being polite
to avoid honesty

I love them
and what began here in me

But home is where I can go,
I must grow elsewhere.

❖ *Florida Overcast*

The sky looks like we're underwater

I don't do drugs so I can
achieve human nobility

I walked in the woods today

I watched the children play

Last night the beach was cold
and large
the water black beyond midnight

what if a comet fell to Earth,
into that ocean?

❖ *In Response: To Heavens Gate': Reflections and Comments from an observer.*

I.

Take a Mason Jar.
Fill it with tap-water and place it
in the sun.
As the water evaporates it will be replaced
by purified, unfiltered,
1000% true Sunlight

—Spiritualized—

Swallow it down,
let the sunlight surround your digestive track,
Let it shine there beautifully.

Keep drinking until your head
is buzzing and your ears
        are spinning.

Then jump up and down repeatedly
until it mixes with your soul.

II.

Comet,   Comet,
meteor
shooting star
-satellites falling.

Bring your black top Nike's
and wear your Adidas shirts—
accept a $1.25 for the endorsement

Shed your hair and dance naked
on the back porch of your summer mansion.

Three plastic bags all in a row.

Comet,   Comet,
meteor
shooting star
-satellites falling.

III.

Bloody your noses
cut your wrists and sing songs
as your keepsakes
and be happy in Videotaped memorial.

Mrs. Bopp is coming

Angels Falling
Heaven Opening

All our songs are sung and are jokes are spo-
ken.

Applesauce at midnight
and flight attendant sick sacks in place.

Heavens gate opening
Souls dancing
Songs singing

And souls are lost to Cosmic bartenders in the
sky,
letting air stir in the nostrils of dead men.

Mrs. Bopp keeps going
—Never giving pause—

IV.

Do your mothers weep?
Into silent cups of coffee
as your pictures flash onto
the screen?
As 'Good Morning America'
tells of your tragedy…

And moves onto the Timothy McVeigh trial.

Do your fathers scream!
At comets and stars hanging
ignorantly in the sky.

Do you die!
Again and again and again
as the Gate opens
—   and you miss the door.

Spinning into fiery oblivion,
passing away into the cold of night.

❖ *Road Trip: New York City, Winter 2000*

do you ever,
etch your heart
onto coffee stained napkins
and dream that your
romances are Calvin Klein ads.

in the waking world
sometimes I realize
that I have forgotten
how to fly.

I am constantly appalled by hypocrisy.

My hypocrisy is a constant.

❖ *Love letter to a cousin, age 9*

To Brianna Lee Hubbard, whose name is sweet
magic on my lips as it drops from those cliffs
so effortlessly; I do declare with joyful heart
and quickened pulse, all rights, duties and obli-
gations
of love that accompany the title of friend and
family.

I am Jason Hubbard Derr.
And with memories ear I do hear the whis-
pered
laugh of a smiled giggle on a summers after-
noon.
My brain aches as memories fill the void your
absence has placed in my mind.

They are a storm manifest, rushing into the
aching vacuum
on Mercury's feet.

I am a twig.
Helpless among the downpour.

Real time memories balloon up into life sized
images.
I see a back yard circus and two tightrope
walkers
following a line etched into the grass over a pit
with no net.

I hear sighs of disgust and exhaust and mut-
tered words of 'your dumb'
and 'your so stupid' that do fade and shift like
shadows at noon
onto new meanings with new faces.

Hidden behind syllables and stashed behind
letters are new
words.
'I LOVE YOU' etched on the heart in a perma-
nent ink.

I hold in my hand other thoughts, I grasp
tightly, praying
that none escape through my fingers.

Silly grins and loud laughs as I do a trade-
marked

'Jason Move'.
Funny looking hats hang loosely from our
heads as we again
mount a giant tree that held the world by it's
root's.

I remember a girl who could not hug, grasping
my arm in an
enduring moment that was suspended between
seconds and
hung there like a rock so beautiful.

I awake now, and go into my day, holding onto
these
memories like an anchor.

I pause and look toward heaven and utter these
words for you.
"Lord because I love her I ask: Watch her, help
her, and guide her!"

❖ *The Preservation of Memory as Souvenir*

I want to preserve memory
as a souvenir

dusted on the top shelf
and trapped in old photographs

(we were so much younger
then)

with dreams ridding in our
back pockets

If I don't look in the mirror
I will forget my own face.

❖ *Road Trip: Florida to Virginia (in transit) 2000*

In the morning
fog hangs by the road like
a gauze or shadow

giving the impression of a ghost town.

We only have headlights
in the early mornings.

There is only the road.

❖ *God and Me: I'm naked.*

If we had both been naked,
not in wild abandon but just standing there,
or had God not been there,
say on vacation or out to lunch,
there would have been problems.

But we were both clothed,
in that awkward, innocent kind
of way.

And God sat in a chair
keeping up a steady conversation
about the weather and school and
my mother and what my plans were,
smoking his pipe.

I think we noticed each other,
she and I,
in a 'spotlight of the mind'
kind of way.

When God asked us to tea
we both answered 'Yes' very nervously,
and we seemed to get more tea on us
than in.

And God:
        What did the old man have to do
        with this?
        What of the Kid?
        And the Scholar?

And what is behind 'like' and 'dates'
and 'love' and 'lust' and 'sex'
and 'children'.

And
        He
                Just
                        Chuckles
                                To him self.

And he smokes his pipe
and laughs.

His old man-wise eyes sparkle,
holding the entire universe.

 # *Desiree*

Desiree eats a wild flower
and paints the sky red

But in her dreams she paint's
it white instead.

❖ *Riverside*

City on the harbor,
drowning the boat lights
in their own reflection,

we watch as Manatees
make love:

And comment on
the suspension of disbelief
in our own lives.

❖ *18*

Scott is wooing a woman,
the costume lady from his play,
a hyperactive 22 year old.

She smiles a lot and can give long
speeches on the psychological state
of the union.

She stayed with us for a four hour
discussion of politics, film and
philosophy.

and Kurt Vonnigut
and pretty much anything by C.S. Lewis

We like to pretend we are deep

Maybe.

Maybe not.

We will see!

❖ *Surprised by Jack*

Sometimes,
when he's not looking,
I will steal lines
from CS Lewis

and eat them.

❖ *February 26, 2000*

Mothers,
in the lost hours
of night,

(with coffee cups,
and candlesticks
at the ready.

with a nervous frown
on their face's)

will try to understand,
and relate their lives
to our own

I'm sure it applies

I'm just not sure how!

❖ *Road Trip: North Carolina—Florida (Summer '98)*

In North Carolina;
we blistered into a cabin
by the beach

It was cold in a way
unique to summer

3, out of 5

I ate clam chowder
for the first time

My parents had their Honeymoon
near here,
and practiced my conception.

In Florida;
palm tree's laced with dust
from back roads

we fished
and swam in the lake.

when the mosquito's came
we went for beer.

❖ *The end of war*

In the last days of the millennium we like to
pretend that we, humans, are kind and wise.
That we have achieved what our parents
couldn't; the end of war.

Or the invention of noble war. This is a falsity.
We just like to pretend this because we make
music or painting's, (so then we must be noble).

We tend to sell our art to finance our war's.

❖ *October-February*

I dream
on stage.

Ross and Angus
argue for my lines.

sometimes I wonder
what my call is.

I have my loves;
but not necessarily
the talent.

by the beach
I feel pulled

the deep-dark
is full of mystery
and wonder.

There is a wall
between my two
worlds,

one that quickly
approaches.

I grind my teeth in
my sleep.

❖ ## *The Education of Brian Bean!*

Huzzah!

Young ones!

Pay your toll
and exit to the
left

—   for your future.

Polish your selves
and put a penny
in your loafers

Smile!
Shake a few hands!

—NETWORK—

Keep your tie straight!

Old Ones!

Disregard your past,
the knowledge you fought
hard to win.

We don't need it!

Do we?

Why would we?
We can crunch numbers
and //.com.me

The past is a convenient
excuse to misunderstand
the future!

Right?

Anyway,
why do I care!
I paid my four dollars
for my education.

So hand me a fistful of
paper and I'll be gone.

❖ *The War Raven*

The War-Raven hides his head
      Dulling his beaks blood-shine,
      wings beat at the
      Midnight forever.

He coos in the ear of the peasant
      boy,
          Trying to force distraction.
To pull him away from the fields of
ripe wheat that vibrate in the cold winter
sun.
      The Peasant Boy whistles a tune of sim-
      ple existence
      that pulsates it's way into the forever-
      now.

The
War-Raven
      Angers inside, pulling
storm clouds to him self, eating the

darkness and absorbing the night.
Pushing into the peasant boy's skull all his
anger at The Farmer.
   Nailing into his brain the rage of a thou-
  sand
nameless generations.
     It courses in his blood,
     a small memory of
     hatred.

But he whistles

   The War-Raven hates now,
   hates forever,
   letting his nakedness

Seduce Him
Seduce Him

'Come to me' the raven whispers to his brain-
streams.
'come to me' and 'Make love to the wind'

'.........'

   The Boy shudders as the Ravens wings
brush
  his

back

The Peasant boy erupts in song.
His lungs focusing the love of his bodies every
cell.

'Upward and Inward'

The Raven clutches inward as a chest pain
                    Tears through his
body.

He falls into the field, tearing open
his skull upon a rock.

In the Farmers field
        Plowed by a simple Peasant Boy.

❖ *Memories Sold: $1.25*

"Memories sold or bought on
street corners, acting in blue bags
of dream.

Pulsating into the harvested moon."

(A Storefront Advertisement)

A Dollar 25 thrown on the counter,
tip-tingling in a metallic musical note.
The old man behind the counter
reminds me of when I was young
and smart.

He gazes at me, winking slightly,
laughing around his pipe.

"One Summers Day, Please!" I ask-beg
with my eyes.

He chokes on his phlegm and stoops
to rummage through a large cardboard
box labeled 'FIX'.

And the man in the corner,
with the top hat and cane
and his face painted like a
skull and his eyes vibrate
with the passion of Forever.

He just laughs!

'Here, here, here—here you go.
a summer day, bought off a man
who went to the beach, don'ch'ya
know. wink wink, nudge'

"Yes,
I know"

I walk back to the painted green street
and load my self-back into my car.
Shooting my self down the alleyways.

I start to think…

so I hatch open the radio,
filling the spaces in my head

with the remnants of pop culture
idolatry.

I take the drug, laying it under
my eye lids.

My bone marrow rebels—

and I see the man with the painted face.

he's in the shadows;
darkness pulled tight against him.

"Are you death?"
—   I see a summers day   —

"I am death?"
—   The beach   —

"Are you here for me?"
—   Children (mine?) laughing in the sand—

"The memories are mine, I paid for them."
—   The hotel, my wife (naked)-

"You can't have them!!!!"
—   Holding her tight, her breath hot on my
back —

"I PAID FOR THEM!"

My voice cannoned at him in vibrant Green.
I spin my wedding band nervously
The angry discolored skin underneath chafing
the sky.

The memories fill me like a new
balloon with a weak string.

"They are mine. I was there. I was him!"
—   The moon over the ocean   -
—   The children in the nocturnal realm

THE REAL!
THE BECOMING!

"He's dead"

"I am Him!"

"Then…. you are dead!"

The memories burn,
 like the nightmare fog
in the morning suns warrior stare.

When death is gone I cry silently
into my bottle of sleep.